Modern Middle East

Blane Conklin, Ph.D.

Publishing Credits

Historical Consultants
Jeff Burke, M.Ed.
Fernando Pérez, M.A.Ed.

Editors
Wendy Conklin, M.A.
Torrey Maloof

Editorial Director
Emily R. Smith, M.A.Ed.

Editor-in-Chief
Sharon Coan, M.S.Ed.

Creative Director
Lee Aucoin

Illustration Manager
Timothy J. Bradley

Publisher
Rachelle Cracchiolo, M.S.Ed.

Teacher Created Materials

5301 Oceanus Drive
Huntington Beach, CA 92649-1030
http://www.tcmpub.com
ISBN 978-0-7439-0674-6
© 2008 Teacher Created Materials, Inc.
Reprinted 2012
BP 5028

Table of Contents

Three Religions in the Middle East

Most people in the Middle East are Muslims (MUHZ-luhmz). Their religion is called Islam. There are also Christians from many different backgrounds. Judaism is another religion in the Middle East. Most religious Jews live in the country of Israel, but there are some Jewish people in other countries as well.

The Cradle of Civilization

Two important ancient civilizations were born in the Middle East. Ancient Egypt grew up around the Nile River. This is the longest river in the world. Ancient Mesopotamia grew up around the Tigris and Euphrates rivers. This area is modern-day Iraq.

Current map of the Middle East

4

A Story of Conflict

The Middle East is one of the most complicated areas in the world. It is the birthplace of three major religions: Judaism (JOO-dee-izuhm), Christianity, and Islam (is-LAWM). And, it is a bridge between three continents: Africa, Europe, and Asia.

The modern history of the Middle East is a story of **conflict**. These conflicts come from three main issues. First, the nation of Israel (IZ-ree-uhl) was formed in 1948. This sparked conflict with those who already lived in the region. Second, **religious extremism** (ik-STREEM-izuhm) causes many conflicts. Some people use their beliefs as an explanation for violence. Third, there is a large amount of oil in the Middle East. Nations around the world rely on this oil supply. So, this often causes conflict, too.

Events in the Middle East affect us all. People around the world pay close attention to what happens there. Because of this, it is important that we try to understand the Middle East.

Oil field pumps are a common sight in some parts of the Middle East. This part of the world produces the most oil.

Israel: A New Place in the World

The modern nation of Israel began in 1948. It had been almost 1,900 years since the Jewish people had a country of their own. Jewish people had been mistreated and killed in many countries around the world. So, they fled from these places. For a long time, they had nowhere to go.

These Jewish families had nowhere to live in 1920.

After World War II, the United Nations (UN) got involved. The UN **partitioned**, or divided, Palestine (PAL-uh-stine) into two parts. There was a Jewish section and a Palestinian (pal-uh-STIN-ee-uhn) section. On May 14, 1948, Israel became its own country. The Palestinian land came under the control of other Arab nations. Many Jewish people flooded into the new country. There, they built cities and planted farms and orchards.

However, life in Israel has not been peaceful. Israel has been in many wars. The Palestinians fight against the Israelis (iz-RAY-leez) to reclaim the land they feel the UN took from them. The country also has many Arab (AIR-uhb) neighbors who oppose the Israelis being there.

Oil r
Che
Heav
Met
Ship

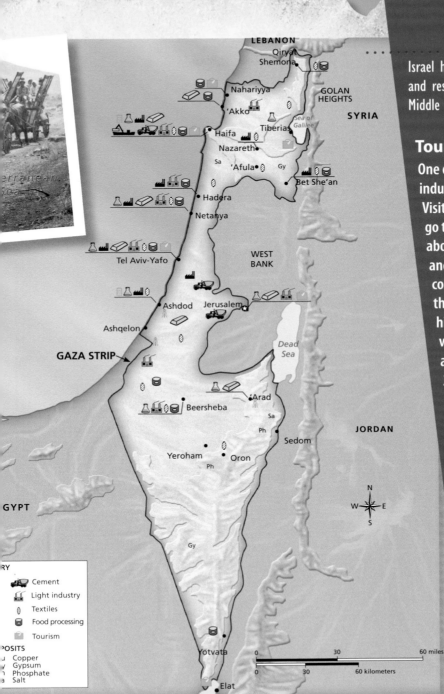

Israel holds valuable land and resources in the Middle East.

Tourism in Israel

One of the most important industries in Israel is tourism. Visitors from all around the world go to Israel to see places they read about in the Bible. Jerusalem has ancient places of worship and colorful markets. Throughout the country there are interesting historical sites. Many Christians visit the town of Bethlehem around Christmas time. A 2,000 year old fishing boat at the Sea of Galilee draws visitors. They also enjoy the Roman ruins in the area. The country's climate is pleasant, and there are four seas to swim in. People use the mineral-rich mud from the Dead Sea for skin treatments. They even sell this special mud to visitors.

Map labels

LEBANON
Qiryat Shemona
GOLAN HEIGHTS
Nahariyya
'Akko
SYRIA
Tiberias
Sea of Galilee
Haifa
Nazareth
Sa
'Afula
Gy
Bet She'an
Hadera
Netanya
WEST BANK
Tel Aviv-Yafo
Ashdod
Jerusalem
Ashqelon
Dead Sea
GAZA STRIP
Arad
Sa
Beersheba
Ph
Sedom
JORDAN
Yeroham
Oron
Ph
EGYPT
Gy
Yotvata
Elat
Mediterranean Sea

N
W E
S

0   30   60 miles
0   30   60 kilometers

Legend

RY / INDUSTRY
- Cement
- Light industry
- Textiles
- Food processing
- Tourism

DEPOSITS
- Copper
- Gypsum
- Phosphate
- Salt

Israel at War

A Time for War

In 1973, an attack was launched on Yom Kippur (YOHM kip-POUR). This is a religious holiday when Jewish people are not to do any work. They fast and pray during the day. However, when Israel was attacked, the nation had to defend itself.

Leading Israel

Golda Meir (meh-IR) worked in Israel's government for more than 25 years. She served in many different positions, including ambassador to the Soviet Union. In 1969, she became the prime minister. On October 6, 1973, the Yom Kippur War broke out. Israel was not prepared to fight this war. They were losing ground. Meir asked the United States for support. With U.S. help, the tide turned, and the war ended. In April 1974, Meir resigned as prime minister.

Since it became a nation in 1948, Israel has fought many wars. The first one was a war against five other nations. The nations were Egypt, Syria (SEAR-ee-uh), Lebanon (LEB-uh-nuhn), Iraq (ih-RAWK), and Jordan. It might have seemed like a long shot, but Israel won that war. The Israeli army was very strong.

In 1956, Israel fought with Egypt for control of the Sinai Peninsula (SYE-nye puh-NIN-suh-luh). This peninsula is between Egypt and Israel. Israel did not win this war.

In 1967, the five nations attacked Israel again. Israel won this war in just six days! So, they named it the Six Day War. Because they won, Israel took control of some new land. In the North, Israel took control of the Golan Heights (GO-lawn HITES) from Syria. In the South, it took the Sinai Peninsula and the Gaza Strip from Egypt. In the central region, it took control of the West Bank from Jordan.

In all of these wars, Egypt was the strongest enemy that Israel faced. Soon, Egypt would be the first Arab nation to hold serious peace talks with Israel.

Israeli armed forces fight during the Yom Kippur War.

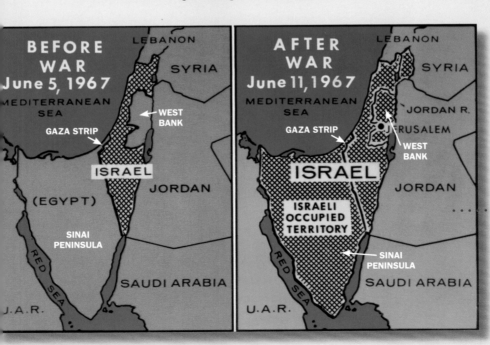

Israel's territory grew after winning the Six Day War. Since then, Israel has changed again.

Egypt and Israel Make History

In 1978, United States president Jimmy Carter asked two leaders to come to a meeting. Their countries had been enemies for a long time. One leader was Anwar Sadat (AHN-whar suh-DOT), the Egyptian president. The other was Israel's prime minister, Menachem Begin (muh-NAW-kuhm BAY-ghin). They met in the United States at the president's vacation spot, Camp David. The two leaders agreed to a peace treaty named the Camp David Accords (uh-KORDZ). So in 1979, Egypt became the first Arab country to make peace with Israel.

The agreement between Egypt and Israel was very important. The two leaders received the Nobel Peace Prize for their work. Still, not everyone was happy with them. Islamic (iz-LAWM-ik) religious extremists were unhappy. They did not want any Arab country to make treaties with Israel.

Anwar Sadat (left) shakes hands with Menachem Begin (right). U.S. President Jimmy Carter watches the two men.

Suez Canal ferry boat

Egyptian President Anwar Sadat

Getting Two Seas Together

Egypt is on the coast of two large seas: the Mediterranean (med-uh-tuhr-RAY-nee-uhn) Sea and the Red Sea. The two seas are separated by land. The Suez (SOO-ez) Canal was built in the 1860s to connect the seas. This is an important shortcut for ships in the area.

Getting Two Leaders Together

When Sadat and Begin met at Camp David, they did not want to talk to each other. President Carter had to act like a shuttle bus going back and forth between the two men.

Just three years later, Sadat was watching a parade pass in front of him. One of the trucks in the parade stopped. Soldiers on the truck lifted their guns. They shot and killed Sadat in the middle of the parade. The shooters were Islamic extremists.

Choosing Sides

The United States often supports one side in a conflict. Sometimes, it is hard for the public to know why a certain side was chosen. The United States supported the shah of Iran because he helped the Middle East remain stable. When the area is stable, the price of oil stays low.

Did You Know?

Many people in the Middle East are Arabs. However, the people in Iran are Persians (PUHR-zhuhnz). The official language of Iran is Farsi (FAR-see).

This stop sign is in Farsi.

This is Shah Pahlavi and President Jimmy Carter.

Islamic Revolution in Iran

Iran (ih-RAN) is another country in the Middle East. It is very rich in oil. In spite of this, in the 1970s, the people there got poorer and poorer. At the same time, the ruler of Iran got richer and richer. His name was Shah Mohammed Reza Pahlavi (mo-HAM-muhd rih-ZAY PAH-luh-vee). The people turned to their religious leaders for help.

One religious leader was Ayatollah Khomeini (eye-uh-TOLL-uh ko-MAY-nee). He was an Islamic extremist. He said he wanted to improve the living conditions in Iran. This sounded good to many people. So they listened to him.

In 1979, the shah became sick with cancer. He left Iran to get better medical treatment. When he was away, Khomeini led a group that took over Iran. The Islamic extremists did not let the shah return. They started a **revolution** (rev-uh-LOO-shuhn). Khomeini said the Islamic religion would be the new law of the land.

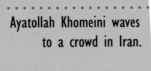

Ayatollah Khomeini waves to a crowd in Iran.

Protesters burn the American flag on top of the U.S. embassy in Iran.

A Crisis in Iran

When the Islamic rulers took over Iran, there were some big changes. Some Iranians (ih-RAY-nee-uhnz) showed how much they hated the United States. They held protests and burned United States flags.

On November 4, 1979, Islamic extremists surrounded the American **embassy** (EM-buh-see). This embassy was in Tehran (tay-RAN), the capital of Iran. The protestors broke in and took 90 American people **hostage**. Some hostages were soon released. But 52 people remained captive for more than a year.

This hostage crisis was a hard time for the United States. Many people tied yellow ribbons around trees in their front yards. They hoped these hostages would be coming home soon. Every day people watched the reports and hoped for some good news. President Carter made plans for a secret rescue. But the helicopter he sent there crashed in the desert. Eight American soldiers died in that crash.

The hostage crisis finally ended on January 21, 1981. This long ordeal lasted for 444 days.

Playing with Fire
Nuclear (NOO-klee-uhr) power is often in the news. Nuclear energy can be used for peaceful purposes, like producing electricity. But it can also be used to make dangerous weapons.

Behind the Scenes
Many years later, it was learned that the hostages were freed after the United States made a deal with the kidnappers. In exchange for the release of hostages, the United States sent weapons to Iran. Iran needed these weapons in their war with Iraq.

These Americans were held hostage by Iranians for more than a year.

Getting from Here to There

Some Palestinians work in Israel. They go through checkpoints when they enter Israel. Soldiers check their IDs to make sure that they have work permits. When there is trouble in the occupied territories, these checkpoints are often closed. The Palestinian workers cannot get to work.

Life as a Refugee

Millions of Palestinians live in refugee camps. These overcrowded neighborhoods often lack necessities like water, electricity, and sewers.

: Young Palestinians riot in the streets.

The Palestinian Struggle for Independence

Palestinians are Arab people from the area of the Middle East called Palestine. Palestine is on the eastern edge of the Mediterranean Sea. There was no independent country on this land for hundreds of years.

In 1948, this land became the nation of Israel. Jewish people from around the world moved to Israel. This caused tensions with the Palestinians who already lived there. Many Palestinians had to leave their homes. They became **refugees** (ref-you-JEEZ).

In the 1970s and '80s, the conditions for the Palestinian people only became worse. Many Palestinians lived in areas taken over by Israel. These were called **occupied territories**. This means the Israeli army ruled there. These occupied territories were the West Bank and the Gaza Strip. The Israelis did not allow the Palestinians to govern themselves.

In 1987, an uprising began. It was called the **intifada** (in-tuh-FAW-duh), or awakening. Many young Palestinians filled the streets day after day. They threw rocks at Israeli soldiers to express their anger.

Palestinian refugees

A Time for Peace: The Oslo Accords

After seven years of the intifada, Israeli and Palestinian leaders decided they needed to end it. The year was 1993, and these leaders met to talk about peace. Yasir Arafat (YAH-sir AIR-uh-fat) represented the Palestinians. Yitzhak Rabin (YIT-sock rah-BEAN) was the prime minister of Israel.

They met in Oslo, Norway. So they named their agreement the Oslo (OZ-low) Accords. The agreement allowed the Palestinians to make their own rules. In return, the Palestinians had to stop attacking Israel.

Coming to this agreement was difficult. These leaders received a special honor, the Nobel

Palestinians celebrate the signing of the Oslo Accords.

Yasir Arafat, Israeli Foreign Minister Shimon Peres, and Yitzhak Rabin received the Nobel Peace Prize.

The Nobel Prize

Nobel prizes are awarded every year for many different categories. The categories include science, mathematics, peace, and economics. The award is named after Alfred Nobel, a Swedish inventor.

A National Celebration

The Oslo Accords were signed in Washington, D.C. On that day, Palestinian villages were alive with excitement. People lined up on the streets. Cars sped by with boys hanging out. Some young men even stood on cars waving Palestinian flags.

Peace Prize. Every year this award is given to people who work hard for peace. Unfortunately, many people on both sides were not happy with the agreement.

Some Palestinians continued to fight against Israel. Some Israelis were angry with their leader for meeting with Arafat. One of these was a Jewish religious extremist. Sadly, he shot and **assassinated** (uh-SAS-suh-nay-ted) Prime Minister Rabin.

If These Walls Could Talk . . .

A visitor to the Old City in Jerusalem can pay a small fee to walk around on top of the walls of the city. These walls were built in the Middle Ages on top of the ruins of older walls.

The Dome of the Rock

The Dome of the Rock is very important to three different religious groups. Muslims believe it is where Muhammad went up to heaven and then returned to Earth. Christians and Jews believe Abraham almost sacrificed his son, Isaac, there.

A man reads a Torah (TORE-uh) scroll at the Wailing Wall. The Torah is the religious book of Judaism.

This picture shows the high walls surrounding the Old City in Jerusalem.

The Holy City of Jerusalem

Jerusalem (jeh-ROO-suh-luhm) is a city in Israel. There are three main parts to this ancient city. There is the modern Jewish city. This area is like many other cities in the world. And, there is East Jerusalem. This is home to many Palestinian people.

The third part of Jerusalem is the Old City. This part of the city is surrounded by a high wall that was built in the Middle Ages. The Old City is divided into four quarters. Different groups live in each quarter. These groups include Muslims, Jewish people, Christians, and Armenians (are-MEE-nee-uhnz).

Jerusalem is an important city to many people. It is the most holy city in Judaism. The Wailing Wall is in the Old City. It is a place of prayer for Jewish people. The wall is all that remains of an ancient Jewish temple built by King Solomon. Jerusalem is important to Christians, as well. They believe that Jesus spent his last days on Earth here. Muslims have an important **mosque** (MAWSK) in Jerusalem. It is named the Dome of the Rock. Muslims believe this is where the **prophet** Muhammad (moh-HAHM-uhd) rose to heaven.

Both Palestinians and Israelis claim Jerusalem as their capital city. They have not yet agreed on how they will solve this problem.

The Muslim Dome of the Rock

Saudi Arabia and Black Gold

The ground in the Middle East holds more than half of the oil in the world. Saudi Arabia (SAW-dee uh-RAY-bee-uh) has the most of any country. Iraq, Kuwait (koo-WAYT), and Iran also have large amounts of oil. This oil gives these countries a lot of power and money. Saudi Arabia is among the richest countries in the world.

Oil is important to **industrialized** (in-DUHS-tree-uh-lized) countries. These nations depend on oil for gasoline. They also use it to make electricity and heat.

Mecca is in Saudi Arabia. It is the center of the Muslim world.

There are many oil refineries, like this one, in Saudi Arabia.

Conflicts in the Middle East affect the cost of oil. Nations there try to work together to control prices. In the 1970s, they decided to send very little oil to the United States. They were mad that the United States was supporting Israel during one of its wars. All of a sudden, gasoline was hard to get. Gas prices soared.

Oil was also at the heart of the Persian Gulf War in the early 1990s. Oil is still one of the reasons the United States is involved with the Middle East.

September 11, 2001

Most of the men who carried out the attacks against the United States on September 11, 2001, were from Saudi Arabia. They were Islamic religious extremists. Their leader, Osama bin Laden, grew up in a wealthy Saudi Arabian family.

Oil in the West

Only two percent of the world's oil reserves are in the United States. Some of them are found in Texas and the Gulf of Mexico. The rest is in Alaska.

The Persian Gulf War

This symbol represents the United Nations.

In 1990, the **dictator** of Iraq was Saddam Hussein (suh-DAHM hoo-SAYN). Hussein invaded Kuwait. Kuwait is a small country that borders Iraq. Kuwait is a much smaller country, but it has almost as much oil as Iraq. Hussein wanted to take control of Kuwait's oil to make him richer. The United Nations warned Hussein not to attack Kuwait. But, Hussein ignored the UN.

President George H. W. Bush led a group of nations to fight Hussein. They sent warships, tanks, and soldiers to Kuwait. In just a few days, Hussein's army was defeated. His soldiers left Kuwait, but they did not leave quietly. They set fire to Kuwait's oil wells and destroyed everything in their paths.

The UN had to punish Hussein for what he did. So they sent inspectors into his country. These inspectors tried to make sure that Hussein would not plan any more attacks.

Nations United?

The United Nations was formed after World War II. It is made up of representatives from nations around the world. This organization tries to help nations solve their problems peacefully. However, this is not always an easy job.

Presidents and the Middle East

Ever since President Carter, every U.S. president has played a big role in Middle East events.

These oil wells in Kuwait were set on fire by Hussein's army.

Kuwait City before
the Persian Gulf War

The War in Iraq

In 1998, Hussein made a bold move. He decided to kick out the UN inspectors who were watching him. People worried that he was making nuclear weapons. By 2003, some world leaders felt Hussein was up to no good. President George W. Bush led several nations in an attack on Iraq.

At first, the war seemed to be easy for the United States. Soldiers captured Baghdad (BAG-dad), the capital of Iraq. On December 13, 2003, Hussein was found and put in prison.

A U.S. general speaks to his troops in Iraq.

Saddam Hussein's trial was in Baghdad.

On Trial

Hussein was put on trial in Iraq for crimes he committed against his own people. The trial was conducted by Iraqis. Hussein was convicted of his crimes and was hanged in 2006.

A Queen Makes a Difference

Queen Rania of Jordan was born to Palestinian parents. She went to school in both Kuwait and Egypt. She is a businesswoman and has committed her life to making the world a better place for women and children. Since 2006, she has been working with the United Nations Children's Fund to help children in Iraq. Iraqi children need health care, clean water, better living conditions, and schooling. She is helping these children get the help they so desperately need.

At this point, some people thought the hardest part of the war was over. But, the war did not end so easily. As of 2007, there were still soldiers fighting in Iraq. Most of the fighting is against Islamic extremists.

No one ever found the weapons that people feared Hussein was making. However, he was a ruler who killed and tortured his own people. The people of Iraq are trying to form a new government and want to live in peace.

Queen Rania

Helping Others Understand

Elizabeth Halaby was born in Washington, D.C. Her family was Arab American. She was educated in the United States. Then, she worked all around the world. She ended up working for the royal airline in Jordan. That is where she met King Hussein. She married the king of Jordan and converted to Islam. She also changed her name to Noor al-Hussein. Throughout their marriage, she was very involved in helping others. Since the king's death, she has served as an expert advisor to the United Nations. She gives speeches about understanding the Middle East. She has spent her life working toward improving life in the Middle East.

A Growing Divide

Draw a line up through the middle of the Red Sea and along the border between Israel and Jordan. These two pieces of the earth's crust are slowly pulling apart. The ocean has poured in and formed the Red Sea. Millions of years from now, Israel and Jordan will pull further apart. And, the Red Sea will become even larger.

Always in the News

The Middle East is in the news every day. Sadly, much of the news is about war and violence. These events often have to do with the nation of Israel. This homeland for Jewish people has been a source of many wars.

Other news in the Middle East is because of religious extremism. When some people follow their religious beliefs, others can get hurt. Conflicts also come from the presence of oil in the region. The world needs the Middle East for its oil.

The Middle East is made up of different cultures. This mix of people and traditions can bring conflict. Many people have lived, worked, and died for the cause of peace in the Middle East.

Today, our world seems a little smaller, and the Middle East seems a little closer. What happens there affects many people in the world. And so, it is important that we try to understand the Middle East.

This Middle Eastern family celebrates together.

The Red Sea, located at the very bottom of this map, will continue to grow over time.

Glossary

assassinated—murdered by surprise attack; usually a prominent person for political reasons

conflict—a fight, battle, or war between people or groups of people

dictator—a single ruler of a country who has complete control

embassy—a location within a country's capital where the representative of a foreign country lives

hostage—a person who is captured and held in order for the hostage taker to get something he or she wants

industrialized—a country that has lots of factories, uses a lot of electricity, and has many automobiles

intifada—an Arabic word meaning "awakening"; refers to the Palestinian uprising from 1987–1993 against Israel's occupation

mosque—a Muslim place of worship

nuclear—a type of energy that can produce a powerful explosion by the splitting of an atom

occupied territories—Palestinian areas occupied by the Israeli army: West Bank and Gaza Strip

partitioned—divided; broken into parts

prophet—leader of a religious group who passes along God's will

refugees—people who are forced to flee their homes and live somewhere else

religious extremism—the use of religious beliefs to justify violence against other people

revolution—a change in a nation's government without an election

Index

Image Credits